BURRITO LOVERS COOK BOOK

FANTASTIC FLAVORFUL FILLINGS!

GOLDEN WEST PUBLISHERS

Printed in the United States of America
5th Printing © 2008

ISBN13: 978-1-885590-95-4
ISBN10: 1-885590-95-4

Golden West Publishers
4113 N. Longview Ave.
Phoenix, AZ 85014, USA
(602)265-4392
(800)658-5830

For free sample recipes for every Golden West cookbook, visit:
www.goldenwestpublishers.com

HOW TO FOLD A BURRITO

1. Place filling about halfway between the center of the tortilla and the edge nearest you.

2. Fold the edge of the tortilla nearest you securely over the filling.

3. Fold the sides to close each end that was left open by the first fold.

4. Finish by rolling the tortilla away from you until it is completely closed.

INTRODUCTION

A burrito is a great way to eat an incredible variety of fillings wrapped in tasty tortillas.

From beans to meat, poultry and seafood, burritos run the gamut from simple to sublime. Stuffed with your favorite savory meat concoctions or filled with tantalizing vegetarian creations, burritos fill our need for tasty, hearty comfort food that is both easy to prepare and easy to eat. And we've even got dessert burritos for you!

A word about tortillas: In today's supermarkets, grocery and specialty stores, a fantastic array of tortillas and wraps are available for adventurous consumers. From basic flour and whole-wheat to spinach and chile, the varieties are colorful as well as flavorful.

The variety of tortilla sizes can be quite confusing—one company's burrito-size tortillas may only be as large as another's fajita-size tortillas—and extra-large by one manufacturer's standards may just match the medium size of another's. The majority of the recipes in *Burrito Lovers Cook Book* call for large flour tortillas (10- to 14-inches in diameter).

There is an art to making great burritos. Fill your tortillas too full at your own risk! Too much filling and the tortilla won't fold properly—too little filling and you'll be eating mostly tortilla. Be creative and find out what works best for you.

SAUCES, SALSAS AND GUACAMOLES

GREEN CHILE SAUCE

1 lb. **Tomatoes**
8 fresh, roasted and peeled **New Mexico Green
   Chiles**, chopped
1 **Onion**, chopped
1-2 cloves **Garlic**, chopped
2 cups **Vegetable Broth**
1/2 tsp. **Salt**
1/4 tsp. **Cumin**
1/4 tsp. **Oregano**

Husk and wash tomatillos. Slice into wedges. In a large saucepan combine tomatillos, chiles, onion, garlic, broth and seasonings. Bring to a boil, reduce heat and simmer for 20 minutes. Pour into blender and pulse to desired consistency.

Makes approximately 4 cups.

RED CHILE SAUCE

8 dried **Red Chile Pods**
2 cloves **Garlic**, chopped
1 **Onion**, chopped
Water
2 tbsp. **Flour**
2 cups **Water**
1 tsp. **Oregano**
1/4 tsp. **Cumin**
1/2 tsp. **Salt**

Wash chiles, remove stems and seeds (leave seeds if you prefer a hotter sauce.) Place chiles, garlic and onion in a pot and cover with water. Bring to a boil, reduce heat and cook for 45 minutes. Drain water. Place chiles, garlic, onion and flour in a blender and purée till smooth. Pour into saucepan, add 2 cups water and seasonings. Cook over medium heat, stirring constantly, until sauce is thick and bubbly.

Makes 3 cups.

JALAPEÑO SALSA

3 **Tomatoes**, diced
1 can (8 oz.) **Tomato Sauce**
2 fresh **Jalapeños**, seeded and diced
2 cloves **Garlic**
1/2 **Onion**, diced
1/4 cup fresh **Cilantro**, chopped
1/2 tsp. **Salt**

Combine all ingredients in a glass bowl and chill for at least four hours.

Makes 4 cups.

CILANTRO SALSA

1 can (15 oz.) **Italian Plum Tomatoes**, drained and
   chopped
1 can (8 oz.) **Tomato Sauce**
1/4 cup fresh **Cilantro**, finely chopped
1 can (4 oz.) **Diced Green Chiles**, drained
1/2 tsp. **Cumin**
1/2 tsp. **Garlic Salt**
1/4 tsp. **Onion Salt**
Pepper to taste

Combine all ingredients in a glass bowl and chill for at least four hours.

Makes 4 cups.

QUICK AND EASY SALSA

1 can (15 oz.) **Stewed Tomatoes**, crushed
1 can (8 oz.) **Tomato Sauce**
1 can (7 oz.) diced **Green Chiles**
1 can (2 oz) chopped **Black Olives**
1 **Onion**, diced
1/2 tsp. **Garlic Salt**
1/2 tsp. **Sugar**
1/4 tsp. **Cayenne Pepper**
1/4 tsp. **Oregano**

Combine all ingredients and chill for several hours before serving.

SALSA VERDE

6 **Anaheim Chiles**, roasted, seeded and diced
1/2 cup fresh **Cilantro**, chopped
1 **Onion**, chopped
1 clove **Garlic,** pressed
1/2 tsp. **Cumin**
1/2 tsp. **Oregano**
1 tbsp. **Lemon Juice**
Salt and **Pepper**, to taste

Place all ingredients in blender and blend until desired thickness. Refrigerate for several hours before serving.

Makes 2 cups.

PICO DE GALLO

3 Tomatoes
4 Jalapeños
1 Onion
1 Green Bell Pepper
2 cloves Garlic
1 bunch fresh Cilantro
1/2 tbsp. Salt
1 tsp. Black Pepper
1/4 cup Cold Water
2 tbsp. Vinegar
1 Lime

On a cutting board, finely chop tomatoes, jalapeños, onion, bell pepper, garlic and cilantro. Place all in glass bowl and mix together. Add salt, pepper, water and vinegar. Squeeze the juice from the lime into the mixture and mix thoroughly. Chill before serving.

About Pico de Gallo

Spanish for "rooster's beak," Pico de Gallo (pee-koh day guy-yoh) is a relish made of finely chopped ingredients. This condiment was so named because it was once purportedly eaten with the thumb and finger, an action that resembles a rooster's pecking beak.

Guacamole

2 ripe **Avocados**
1 tsp. **Lemon Juice**
1 **Onion**, chopped
1 clove **Garlic,** minced
2 tbsp. **Diced Green Chiles**
1 tsp. **Salt**
1/4 tsp. **Pepper**
2 tbsp. **Mayonnaise**

In a glass bowl, mash avocados until creamy. Mix in lemon juice. Add onion, garlic, green chiles, salt and pepper and mix thoroughly. Add mayonnaise and stir or whip to a creamy texture. Chill for 30 minutes and serve.

Spicy Guacamole

3 ripe **Avocados**
1/2 **Onion**, diced
1 fresh **Jalapeño**, seeded and diced
1 tbsp. **Lime Juice**
2 tbsp. **Mayonnaise**
1/2 tsp. **Hot Pepper Sauce**
1 **Tomato**, chopped

Combine all ingredients, except tomato. Blend until smooth; fold in chopped tomato. Use immediately.

BREAKFAST BURRITOS

SUNRISE BURRITOS

1 can (16 oz.) Refried Beans
1 can (4 oz.) diced **Green Chiles**
6 **Eggs**
3/4 cup **Salsa**
1/3 cup chopped fresh **Cilantro**
6 large **Flour Tortillas**
3/4 cup shredded **Monterey Jack Cheese**
1 cup **Plain Non-Fat Yogurt**
Orange Wedges

In a skillet, over medium heat, combine beans and chiles until bubbly hot. In a bowl, beat eggs, 1/4 cup salsa and cilantro. Push beans to one side of skillet and pour egg mixture onto cleared side; stir occasionally until eggs are set (about 3 minutes). Warm tortillas and equally divide beans, eggs and cheese onto each tortilla. Fold into burritos. Serve seam side down on warm plates and top with additional salsa, yogurt and orange wedges.

Serves 6.

SPUDS BURRITOS

3 tbsp. **Vegetable Oil**
1 **Onion**, chopped
1 clove **Garlic**, minced
3 tbsp. diced **Green Chiles**
2 **Russet Potatoes**, cubed and cooked
1/3 cup chopped fresh **Cilantro**
1 tsp. **Chili Powder**
1 tsp. **Cumin**
6 **Eggs**, lightly beaten
6 large **Flour Tortillas**
Salt and **Pepper**
Salsa

Heat oil in skillet and sauté onion and garlic until onion is translucent; add green chiles and potatoes; continue to sauté until potatoes are browned. Add cilantro, chili powder and cumin. Heat thoroughly, stirring occasionally. Pour eggs over potato mixture and continue to cook, using a spatula to lift firm portions allowing uncooked eggs to flow beneath. Cook to desired consistency. Warm tortillas and scoop equal amounts onto each tortilla, seasoning as desired with salt, pepper and salsa. Fold into burritos.

Serves 6.

Cooking Tortillas

*Traditionally, tortillas are cooked on a round,
dry earthenware griddle called a "comal."*

GOOD MORNING BURRITOS

1 **Potato**, boiled
2 tsp. **Vegetable Oil**
3 tbsp. diced **Green Chiles**
1/3 cup shredded **Cheddar Cheese**
2 large **Flour Tortillas**
Salsa

Dice potato and brown in oil in a heated skillet. Stir in chiles and cheese. Fill warmed tortillas and fold into burritos. Serve with salsa.

Serves 2.

HASH BROWN BURRITOS

2 tbsp. **Vegetable Oil**
1/2 **Onion**, diced
1/2 **Green Bell Pepper**, diced
2 cups frozen **Hash Browns**
2 large **Flour Tortillas**
1/2 cup shredded **Longhorn Cheese**
Salsa

In a heated skillet, add oil and sauté onion, bell pepper and hash browns. Spoon onto warmed tortillas, sprinkle with cheese and fold into burritos. Serve with salsa.

Serves 2.

BUENOS DÍAS BURRITOS

6 **Eggs**
1/4 cup **Milk**
1 tbsp. **Butter**
1 can (4 oz.) diced **Green Chiles**
1/2 cup shredded **Cheddar Cheese**
Dash of **Hot Pepper Sauce**
6 large **Flour Tortillas**
Sour Cream
1 **Avocado**, peeled and sliced

In a medium mixing bowl, combine eggs and milk and beat well. Melt butter in skillet and add eggs; cook over medium heat, stirring occasionally. When eggs are almost set add chiles and cheese. Season with pepper sauce. Cook to desired consistency. Spoon onto warmed tortillas and fold into burritos. Serve with sour cream and avocado slices.

Serves 6.

Did You Know?

Burritos are mostly a northern Mexico phenomenon. Prior to the Spanish conquest of Mexico, tortillas were only made from corn. Wheat flour was introduced by the Spaniards.

CHORIZO BURRITOS

8 oz. **Chorizo**
1 pkg. (16 oz.) frozen **Hash Browns**
1 **Onion**, diced
1 **Green Bell Pepper**, diced
1 **Red Bell Pepper**, diced
6 **Eggs**, beaten
1 cup shredded **Monterey Jack Cheese**
6 large **Flour Tortillas**
Salsa

In a skillet, brown chorizo and drain thoroughly on paper towels. In the same skillet, add hash browns, onion and peppers. Sauté until onions and potatoes are golden. Pour in eggs and scramble until almost set. Return chorizo to skillet and mix with eggs, potatoes and peppers. Sprinkle cheese on top. Spoon mixture onto warmed tortillas and fold burrito-style. Serve with salsa.

Serves 6.

Chorizo

Chorizo is a spicy Mexican sausage that can be made with either beef, pork or veal. When creating chorizo, the meat is "cured" for 72 hours (with a variety of spices, peppers and vinegar). The meat is then cooked and used as a side dish or in combination with other foods.

SOYFUL MORNING BURRITOS

1 tbsp. **Vegetable Oil**
1/2 lb. **Soy Sausage**
1 **Green Bell Pepper,** diced
1 can (4 oz.) sliced **Mushrooms**
6 **Eggs,** lightly beaten
1/2 lb. shredded **Soy Cheese**
Salt and **Pepper**
6 large **Flour Tortillas**
Salsa

In a hot skillet, add oil and fry sausage, bell pepper and mushrooms. Stir in eggs and cook until almost set. Sprinkle in cheese, season to taste and cook to desired consistency. Spoon onto warmed tortillas and fold into burritos. Serve with salsa.

Serves 6.

Soy Sausage?

Soy is a low cost source of a plant-based protein food that has been found to be helpful in reducing heart disease, stroke and cancer. Soy is now available in hundreds of different products, including meat-free soy sausage.

BELL RINGER BURRITOS

4 oz. **Breakfast Sausage**
2 tbsp. minced **Onion**
2 oz. diced **Green Chiles**
1/2 tsp. **Garlic Salt**
1/4 tsp. **Pepper**
4 **Eggs**, beaten
4 large **Flour Tortillas**
4 slices **American Cheese**
Salsa

Crumble sausage into a heated skillet; add onion and sauté until sausage is browned. Add chiles, garlic salt, pepper and eggs. Scramble mixture over medium heat and cook to desired consistency. Spoon cooked egg mixture onto warmed flour tortillas and place cheese slices over top. Fold into burritos. Serve with salsa.

Serves 4.

How to Eat a Burrito

When filled and folded properly, a quality tortilla will allow you the option of eating your burrito out-of-hand, or on a plate, using utensils. The messier the filling, the greater the possibility that you will want to use a plate!

EYE-OPENER BURRITOS

1 **Potato**, diced
1/2 lb. **Sausage**
2 **Jalapeños**, seeded and chopped
1 **Onion**, diced
1 **Red Bell Pepper**, chopped
4 **Eggs**
1/2 tsp. **Garlic Salt**
1/2 tsp. **Cumin**
1/2 tsp. **Cayenne**
1/2 tsp. **Pepper**
6 large **Flour Tortillas**
Salsa
Sour Cream

In a heated nonstick skillet, sauté potato and sausage until sausage is fully cooked and potatoes are browned. Add jalapeños, onion and bell pepper and continue cooking until vegetables are tender. In a medium bowl, beat eggs with spices. Pour eggs over sausage and vegetables. Cook over medium heat stirring occasionally until eggs are desired consistency. Spoon onto warmed flour tortillas. Fold into burritos. Serve with salsa and sour cream.

Serves 6.

BURRITO BAKE

2 cans (16 oz. ea.) **Refried Beans**
1 pkg. (8 oz.) **Cream Cheese**
1 cup shredded **Monterey Jack Cheese**
1/2 tsp. **Garlic Salt**
1/2 tsp. **Chili Powder**
1/2 tsp. **Cumin**
1 **Onion**, minced
10 **Eggs**, beaten
10 large **Flour Tortillas**
1 can (15 oz.) **Enchilada Sauce**
1/2 cup shredded **Longhorn Cheese**
4 **Green Onions**, sliced
Salsa
Sour Cream

In large skillet, combine beans, cream cheese, Jack cheese, garlic salt, chili powder, cumin and onion. Heat thoroughly, stirring occasionally, until cheeses are melted. In a separate oiled skillet, scramble eggs until almost set. Spoon equal amounts of beans and eggs onto each warmed flour tortilla; fold burrito-style. Place burritos, seam side down, side by side in large oiled baking dish. Pour enchilada sauce over all; sprinkle with longhorn cheese and green onions. Bake at 325° for 30 minutes or until bubbly hot. Serve with salsa and sour cream.

Serves 10.

RANCHERO BURRITOS

6 **Eggs**
1/4 cup **Milk**
2 tbsp. **Butter**
1 can (4 oz.) diced **Green Chiles**
3/4 cup diced **Ham**
4 large **Flour Tortillas**
1 cup shredded **Colby-Jack Cheese**
1 **Tomato**, chopped
1 **Avocado**, diced
Salsa

In a medium bowl, beat eggs with milk. Melt butter in a large skillet and pour in eggs, green chiles and ham. Scramble to desired consistency. Spoon into warmed flour tortillas; sprinkle with cheese, tomato and avocado. Fold burrito-style and serve with salsa.

Serves 4.

An Avocado by Any Other Name

The word "avocado" is derived from the Aztec "ahuacatl." When ripe, this pear-shaped fruit (it grows on trees) has the consistency of firm butter and a nut-like flavor. To test for ripeness, hold the avocado in the palm of your hand and gently press with your thumb. If the avocado gives slightly, you've got a winner!

BEAN BURRITOS

REFRIED BEANS

1/2 lb. **Pinto Beans**
4 cups **Water**
1 tsp. **Salt**
1 tsp. **Chili Powder**
1/4 tsp. **Red Pepper Flakes**
1/2 cup finely chopped **Onion**
2 tbsp. **Shortening**

Sort and wash beans. In a large saucepan, add beans and cover with 4 cups water. Bring to a boil, cover tightly and cook for 2 minutes. Remove from heat. Do not remove cover and let soak for 1 hour. Drain and cover with fresh water. Add salt, chili powder, red pepper and onion. Bring to a boil, cover tightly, continue cooking on medium/low, stirring occasionally, for 2 hours, or until beans are tender. Add more water, if necessary, to keep beans from sticking. Place beans in a heavy skillet; add shortening and mash to desired consistency. Heat until bubbly hot.

BASIC BEAN AND CHEESE BURRITOS

1 can (16 oz.) **Refried Beans**
1/4 cup minced **Onion**
1/2 tsp. **Garlic Salt**
1/2 tsp. **Oregano**
1/2 tsp. **Chili Powder**
4 large **Flour Tortillas**
1 cup shredded **Cheddar Cheese**
Salsa or **Hot Sauce**

In a medium saucepan, combine beans, onion and seasonings. Cook over medium heat until bubbly hot. Spoon beans onto warmed tortillas, sprinkle with cheese, add salsa or hot sauce, if desired, and fold burrito-style. Serve with salsa or hot sauce.

Serves 4.

Are Refried Beans Really Re-Fried?

The term "refried" resulted from the Mexican "frijoles refritos," which means "well-fried beans."

Fiesta Bean Burritos

1 can (16 oz.) **Refried Beans**
1 can (2.25 oz.) sliced **Black Olives**
1/2 cup minced **Onion**
1 can (4 oz.) diced **Green Chiles**
4 large **Flour Tortillas**
1 cup shredded **Monterey Jack Cheese**
1 **Tomato**, chopped
1 **Avocado**, peeled and chopped
Hot Sauce

In a medium saucepan, combine beans, olives, onion and green chiles. Cook over medium heat until bubbly hot. Spoon onto warmed tortillas, sprinkle with cheese, tomato, avocado and hot sauce. Fold burrito-style.

Serves 4.

Mexican Cheese

Mexican cheeses are gaining popularity in Southwestern cooking. For burritos, instead of cheddar and Jack cheeses, try Queso Chihuahua or Queso Blanco.

PICANTE BLACK BEAN BURRITOS

1 can (15 oz.) **Black Beans,** rinsed
1/2 cup **Picante Sauce**
1 pkg. (3 oz.) **Cream Cheese**
1/2 cup chopped **Green Bell Pepper**
1/2 tsp. **Garlic Salt**
1/2 tsp. **Cumin**
1/2 tsp. **Oregano**
4 large **Flour Tortillas**
1 cup shredded **Monterey Jack Cheese**
Sour Cream
Salsa

In a medium saucepan, combine black beans, picante sauce, cream cheese, bell peppers, garlic salt, cumin and oregano. Heat until bubbly hot. Spoon onto warmed flour tortillas, top with cheese, fold burrito-style and top with sour cream and salsa.

Serves 4.

BLACK-EYED PEA BURRITOS

1 can (16 oz.) **Black-Eyed Peas**
1 can (4 oz.) diced **Green Chiles**
1/2 cup minced **Onion**
1/2 cup diced **Green Bell Pepper**
1/2 tsp. **Garlic Salt**
1/2 tsp. **Oregano**
1/4 tsp. **Pepper**
1/4 tsp. **Cayenne**
4 large **Flour Tortillas**
1 cup shredded **Colby-Jack Cheese**
Sour Cream
Salsa

In a medium saucepan, mash black-eyed peas and combine with chiles, onion, green bell pepper and seasonings. Heat thoroughly. Spoon onto warmed flour tortillas and sprinkle with cheese. Fold burrito-style and serve with sour cream and salsa.

Serves 4.

ANASAZI BEAN BURRITOS

1 lb. dried **Anasazi Beans**
6 cups **Water**
1/4 cup finely chopped **Onion**
1 clove **Garlic**, crushed
6 slices **Bacon**, chopped
1/4 cup chopped **Green Bell Pepper**
1 tsp. **Chili Powder**
6 large **Flour Tortillas**
1 cup shredded **Cheddar** or **Monterey Jack Cheese**
Sour Cream
Salsa
1 **Avocado**, sliced

In a large saucepan, combine beans and water and simmer gently for 1 + hours or until tender. Drain beans, reserving liquid. In a medium skillet, sauté onion, garlic, green bell pepper and bacon. Add sautéed ingredients to beans and mash all together, adding reserved liquid a little at a time, until mixture is smooth. Heat thoroughly; spoon onto warmed flour tortillas, sprinkle with cheese and fold burrito-style. Serve with sour cream, salsa and avocado slices.

Serves 6.

BEEF BURRITOS

GREEN CHILE BURRITOS

1 lb. **Stew Beef**, cubed
Flour
2 tbsp. **Oil**
1 can (7 oz.) diced **Green Chiles**
2 cloves **Garlic**, minced
1/2 tsp. **Oregano**
1/4 tsp. **Cayenne**
Salt and **Pepper**
4 cups **Beef Stock** or **Water**
6 large **Flour Tortillas**

Dredge beef in flour and brown in oil in a large skillet. Add chiles, garlic and seasonings, stir in stock and simmer for 1 hour, until meat is tender. Spoon onto warmed flour tortillas and fold burrito-style.

Serves 6.

SOUR CREAM BEEF BURRITOS

2 lbs. **Lean Ground Beef**
1 **Onion**, chopped
1 **Green Bell Pepper**, chopped
1 can (7 oz.) diced **Green Chiles**
1/2 tsp. **Chili Powder**
1/4 tsp. **Garlic Salt**
1/4 tsp. **Cumin**
1 pint **Sour Cream**
6 large **Flour Tortillas**
2 cups shredded **Monterey Jack Cheese**

In a large skillet, brown ground beef, onion and bell pepper. Drain if necessary. Add green chiles, seasonings and sour cream. Heat thoroughly, stirring occasionally. Spoon onto warmed flour tortillas, sprinkle with cheese and fold burrito-style.

Serves 6.

GRINGO BEEF BURRITOS

2 lb. **Lean Ground Beef**
1 **Onion**, chopped
1 tsp. **Garlic Powder**
1 can (10.75 oz.) **Cream of Mushroom Soup**
1 can (7 oz.) diced **Green Chiles**
1 can (4 oz.) sliced **Black Olives**
6 large **Flour Tortillas**
2 cups shredded **Cheddar Cheese**
Sour Cream
Salsa

In a large skillet, brown ground beef and onion. Drain if necessary. Sprinkle with garlic powder; stir in soup, green chiles and olives. Simmer for 15 minutes, stirring occasionally. Spoon onto warmed flour tortillas, sprinkle with cheese and fold burrito-style. Serve with sour cream and salsa.

Serves 6.

QUICK BEEF AND BEAN BURRITOS

1 lb. **Lean Ground Beef**
1/2 **Onion**, diced
1 can (15 oz.) **Pinto Beans**, drained
1 cup **Salsa**
1 tbsp. **Chili Powder**
1/2 tsp. **Cumin**
1/2 tsp. **Oregano**
Salt and **Pepper**
4 large **Flour Tortillas**

In a large skillet, brown ground beef and onion. Drain if necessary. Add beans, salsa and seasonings. Simmer for 10 minutes, stirring occasionally. Spoon onto warmed flour tortillas and fold burrito-style.

Serves 4.

Chimichangas!

Also known as a "chimi," the beloved and mysterious chimichanga is really nothing more than a burrito which has been deep-fried. Different theories and claims abound as to the origin of chimichangas. Several restaurant proprietors in Arizona claim to be the inventors of these tasty burrito variations, while some folks credit ranchers in Mexico for the innovation of grilling their burritos in oil.

CROCK POT BURRITOS

1 (4-5 lb.) **Beef Roast**
1 jar (16 oz.) **Salsa**
1 **Onion**, chopped
1 **Green Bell Pepper**, chopped
1 cup **Water** or **Beef Stock**
1/2 tsp. **Garlic Powder**
Salt and **Pepper**
6 large **Flour Tortillas**

Trim excess fat from roast. Place roast in crock pot. Add remaining ingredients (except tortillas); cook 6-8 hours on medium setting. Remove meat from crock pot and shred with a fork. Return shredded beef to crock pot and stir, continuing to heat with lid off until liquid has cooked down to desired consistency. Spoon onto warmed flour tortillas and fold burrito-style.

Serves 6.

PICADILLO BURRITOS

1 tbsp. **Oil**
1 1/2 lbs. **Lean Ground Beef**
1 **Potato**, shredded
1 **Onion**, diced
2 cloves **Garlic**, minced
1 can (4 oz.) diced **Green Chiles**
1 1/2 cups frozen **Peas** and **Carrots**
Salt and **Pepper**
6 large **Flour Tortillas**

In a large skillet, heat oil and brown ground beef, potato, onion and garlic. When meat is browned add green chiles, peas and carrots and seasonings. Lower heat, cover and simmer for 15 minutes. Spoon into warmed flour tortillas and fold burrito-style.

Serves 6.

CORNED BEEF BURRITOS

2 cans (12 oz. each) **Corned Beef**
5 oz. canned **Roast Beef**
1 can (4 oz.) diced **Green Chiles**
1/2 tsp. **Cumin**
6 large **Flour Tortillas**
3 cups shredded **Cabbage**
1 **Tomato**, chopped
1 **Green Bell Pepper**, chopped

In a medium skillet, combine corned beef and roast beef over medium heat. Stir in green chiles and cumin and continue cooking for 10 minutes. Spoon into warmed flour tortillas and fold burrito-style. Serve on a bed of shredded cabbage and top with tomatoes and green bell peppers.

Serves 6.

POPEYE BEEF BURRITOS

1 1/2 lbs. **Lean Ground Beef**
1 **Onion**, chopped
2 tbsp. **Chili Powder**
1 tsp. **Garlic Salt**
1 tsp. **Oregano**
1/2 tsp. **Cumin**
1/2 tsp. **Cayenne**
1 cup **Salsa**
1 pkg. (10 oz.) frozen chopped **Spinach**, defrosted
  and well-drained
1 cup shredded **Monterey Jack Cheese**
6 large **Flour Tortillas**
Sour Cream

In a large skillet, brown ground beef with onion until onion is translucent. Add seasonings, salsa and spinach. Cover and simmer for 10 minutes, stirring occasionally. Sprinkle with cheese and then spoon onto warmed flour tortillas; fold burrito-style. Serve with sour cream.

Serves 6.

CHILE VERDE BURRITOS

2 1/2 lbs. **Lean Ground Beef**
1 can (7 oz.) diced **Green Chiles**
2 cloves **Garlic**, minced
Dash **Tabasco**®
Salt and **Pepper**
8 large **Flour Tortillas**
2 cups shredded **Monterey Jack Cheese**
Black Olives
Shredded **Lettuce**
Diced **Tomatoes**
Avocado Slices
Salsa
Sour Cream

In a skillet, brown ground beef; drain if necessary. Add chiles, garlic, Tabasco, salt and pepper. Heat thoroughly, stirring occasionally. Spoon onto warmed flour tortillas and fold burrito-style. Place seam side down in a 13 × 9 baking dish. Cover with foil and bake at 350° for 15 minutes. Remove foil, sprinkle with cheese and olives and return to oven for an additional 5 minutes. Serve on individual plates, accompanied by lettuce, tomatoes, avocados, salsa and sour cream.

Serves 8.

STEAK BURRITOS

2 tbsp. **Oil**
2 lbs. **Round Steak**, cut into thin strips
1 **Onion**, chopped
2 cloves **Garlic**, minced
1 **Jalapeño**, seeded and chopped
1/4 tsp. **Cumin**
Salt and **Pepper**
1 can (15 oz.) **Stewed Tomatoes**
6 large **Flour Tortillas**
Salsa
Sour Cream

Heat oil in a medium skillet and add steak, onion, garlic and jalapeño. Sauté until onion is translucent; add seasonings, stewed tomatoes (include juice) and boil for 10-15 minutes until liquid is reduced. Spoon onto warmed flour tortillas and fold burrito-style. Serve with salsa and sour cream.

Serves 6.

Fajitas!

Fajitas are assumed to be a Tex-Mex dish where the primary ingredient is marinated, grilled skirt steak. The name is derived from the Spanish word "faja," for "girdle" or "strip." One of the original signature features of this dish is that the meat was cooked over mesquite coals.

Red Chile Burritos

1 1/2 lbs. lean **Chuck Roast**
Water
2 tbsp. **Oil**
1 **Onion**, chopped
2 cloves **Garlic**, minced
1/2 tsp. **Oregano**
1 can (15 oz.) **Enchilada Sauce**
6 large **Flour Tortillas**
Sour Cream

Remove all visible signs of fat from chuck roast and place roast in cooking pot, covered with water. Bring to a boil, reduce heat and cover; simmer until meat is fully cooked. Let cool and cut into bite-size pieces or shred with a fork. In a large skillet, heat oil and sauté meat with onion, garlic and oregano, until onion is translucent. Add enchilada sauce and heat thoroughly. Spoon onto warmed flour tortillas and fold burrito-style. Serve with sour cream.

Serves 6.

MACHACA BURRITOS

1 1/2 lbs. lean **Chuck Roast**
Water
2 tbsp. **Oil**
1 **Onion**, chopped
1 **Green Bell Pepper**, chopped
2 **Tomatoes**, coarsely chopped
1 can (7 oz.) diced **Green Chiles**
1/2 tsp. **Garlic Salt**
1/4 tsp. **Cumin**
1/4 tsp. **Oregano**
6 large **Flour Tortillas**
Lettuce
Salsa
Sour Cream

Remove all visible signs of fat from chuck roast and place roast in cooking pot, covered with water. Bring to a boil, cover, reduce heat and simmer until meat is fully cooked and tender. Allow meat to cool, then shred with a fork. In a large skillet, heat oil and sauté meat, onion and green bell pepper until onion is translucent. Add tomatoes and green chiles, garlic salt, cumin and oregano; cover and simmer for 10 minutes. Spoon onto warmed flour tortillas and fold burrito-style. Serve with lettuce, salsa and sour cream.

Serves 6.

For *enchilada style*, place burritos on oven-proof platter, ladle enchilada sauce over top and sprinkle with shredded cheese. Broil for 1 minute.

PORK BURRITOS

PORK CHALUPA BURRITOS

1 (3 lb) **Pork Roast**
1 lb. **Pinto Beans**, washed
1 **Onion**, chopped
1 can (7 oz.) diced **Green Chiles**
2 cloves **Garlic**, chopped
2 tbsp. **Chili Powder**
1 tbsp. **Cumin**
1 tbsp. **Oregano**
1 tbsp. **Salt**
10 large **Flour Tortillas**

Trim all visible signs of fat from roast and place roast, beans, onion, green chiles, garlic and seasonings in a large pot, Dutch oven or crock pot. Add enough water to cover. Simmer, covered, on low heat until meat is tender (approximately 5-6 hours). Remove bones and break up roast. Continue cooking with lid off until mixture thickens. Spoon onto warmed flour tortillas and fold burrito-style. Serve with desired accompaniments.

Serves 10.

SHREDDED PORK BURRITOS

1 (3 lb.) **Pork Roast**
1 **Onion**, chopped
1 **Red Bell Pepper**, chopped
3 cloves **Garlic**, minced
2 cans (7 oz. ea.) diced **Green Chiles**
1 can (15 oz.) **Stewed Tomatoes**
1 tsp. **Oregano**
1/2 tsp. **Cumin**
1/2 tsp. **Cayenne**
Salt and **Pepper**
10 large **Flour Tortillas**

Trim all visible signs of fat from roast and place roast in large pot or Dutch oven. Cover with water, bring to a boil, lower heat, cover and simmer for 30 minutes. Add onion, bell pepper, garlic, green chiles, tomatoes and seasonings; cover and continue cooking until roast is tender (approximately 3-4 hours). Remove bones and stir with a fork to break up meat. With lid removed, continue cooking until mixture thickens (approximately 15 minutes). Spoon onto warmed flour tortillas and fold burrito-style.

Serves 10.

PORK BURRITOS

3 tbsp. **Oil**
2 lbs. lean **Pork Shoulder**, cut into 1/2-inch cubes
2 cups **Chicken Broth**
1 **Onion**, diced
1 can (4 oz.) diced **Green Chiles**
1/2 tsp. **Garlic Powder**
1/2 tsp. **Cumin**
2 tbsp. **Chili Powder**
Salt and **Pepper**
8 large **Flour Tortillas**
1 cup shredded **Cheddar Cheese**

In a large skillet, heat oil and brown pork cubes. Add chicken broth, onion, green chiles and seasonings. Simmer covered for 1 hour. Remove cover and continue to simmer until sauce thickens. Spoon onto warmed tortillas and sprinkle with cheese. Fold burrito-style. Serve with shredded lettuce and chopped tomatoes.

Serves 8.

ACAPULCO PORK BURRITOS

3 cups cooked **Spanish Rice**
1 can (16 oz.) **Kidney Beans**, drained
1 lb. **Pork Loin** or **Roast**, cooked and diced
2 cups **Salsa**
1 **Red Bell Pepper**, diced
1 **Yellow Bell Pepper**, diced
1 **Green Bell Pepper**, diced
1/2 **Onion**, sliced
2 tbsp. **Oil**
Romaine Lettuce Leaves
8 large **Tortillas**

Combine rice, beans and pork; set aside. In a large skillet, sauté peppers and onion in oil until onion is translucent. Add salsa, then stir in rice/bean/pork mixture. Heat thoroughly. Spoon mixture onto tortillas; place lettuce leaf across center of each tortilla before folding burrito-style.

Serves 8.

What to Look for in a Tortilla

A good tortilla, at room temperature, doesn't crack when it is rolled or folded. When choosing tortillas for burritos, pick those that are soft and pliable yet thick enough to handle generous filling without tearing.

CHICKEN AND TURKEY BURRITOS

CREAMY CHICKEN BURRITOS

2 cups diced cooked **Chicken**
1 **Green Bell Pepper**, chopped
1 can (4 oz.) diced **Green Chiles**
1 pkg. (8 oz.) **Cream Cheese**, cubed
1/2 cup **Salsa**
8 large **Flour Tortillas**
1 lb. Velveeta®, cubed
1/3 cup **Milk**

In a saucepan, combine chicken, bell pepper, green chiles, cream cheese and salsa. Stir over low heat until smooth. Spoon chicken mixture onto warmed flour tortillas and fold burrito style. Place burritos seam side down in a 13 × 9 baking dish. In a saucepan, stir Velveeta and milk together over low heat until smooth. Pour cheese sauce over burritos, cover with foil and bake for 20 minutes at 350°.

Serves 8.

CHICKEN AND RICE BURRITOS

3 cups shredded cooked **Chicken**
1 pkg. (1.25 oz.) **Taco Seasoning**
3/4 cup **Water**
2 tbsp. **Oil**
1 **Onion**, chopped
2 cups cooked **Rice**
1 cup **Peas**
1 **Tomato**, chopped
1 can (8 oz.) **Tomato Sauce**
1/2 tsp. **Garlic Salt**
1/2 tsp. **Pepper**
8 large **Flour Tortillas**
1/2 cup shredded **Cheddar Cheese**
1/4 cup chopped **Green Onions**
Shredded Lettuce
Black Olives
Sour Cream
Salsa
Guacamole

In a large skillet, combine chicken, taco seasoning and water. Bring to a boil, reduce heat and simmer for 10 minutes. Spoon chicken mixture into a bowl, return skillet to stove and heat oil; sauté onion until translucent. Stir in rice, peas, tomato, tomato sauce, garlic salt and pepper. Cover and simmer over low heat for 15 minutes. Add chicken mixture to rice mixture and heat thoroughly, stirring to combine. Spoon onto warmed flour tortillas and fold burrito-style. Place burritos seam side down in a 13 × 9 baking dish; sprinkle with cheese and green onions. Bake at 350° for 7-10 minutes. Serve on beds of shredded lettuce and garnish with olives, sour cream, salsa and guacamole.

Serves 8.

CHICKEN FAJITA BURRITOS

4 **Boneless, Skinless Chicken Breast Halves**, cut into
   strips
2 tbsp. **Lemon Juice**
1/2 tsp. **Garlic Salt**
1/2 tsp. **Oregano**
1/2 tsp. **Pepper**
1/4 tsp. **Cayenne**
3 tbsp. **Oil**
1 **Green Bell Pepper**, cut into strips
1 **Red Onion**, sliced
3/4 cup **Salsa**
8 large **Flour Tortillas**

In a medium bowl, marinate chicken breasts in lemon juice, garlic salt, oregano, pepper and cayenne. Cover and refrigerate for 6 hours or overnight. In a large skillet, heat oil and sauté chicken, bell pepper and onion until chicken is no longer pink. Stir in salsa and continue cooking for 5 minutes. Spoon onto warmed flour tortillas and fold burrito-style.

Serves 8.

CHICKEN ASPARAGUS BURRITOS

4 **Boneless, Skinless Chicken Breast Halves,** cooked
    and shredded or cubed
1 can (4 oz.) diced **Green Chiles**
1 can (10.75 oz.) **Cream of Asparagus Soup**
1 can (4 oz.) sliced **Black Olives**
1 cup **Sour Cream**
1/2 lb. shredded **Cheddar Cheese**
8 large **Flour Tortillas**

In a saucepan, combine all ingredients (except flour tortillas) and simmer over low heat for 15 minutes, stirring occasionally. Spoon onto warmed flour tortillas and fold burrito-style.

Serves 8.

CHICKEN SPINACH BURRITOS

1 pkg. (10 oz.) frozen chopped **Spinach**, thawed and
   drained
1 can (10.75 oz.) **Cream of Chicken Soup**
1 can (7 oz.) diced **Green Chiles**
4 **Boneless, Skinless Chicken Breast Halves**, cooked
   and diced
8 large **Flour Tortillas**
1 cup shredded **Monterey Jack Cheese**
1 can (10.75 oz.) **Cream of Mushroom Soup**
1 cup shredded **Cheddar Cheese**
4 **Green Onions**, sliced
1 can (4 oz.) sliced **Black Olives**

In a saucepan, combine spinach, cream of chicken soup, green chiles and chicken. Simmer over low heat for 15 minutes, stirring occasionally. Spoon onto warmed flour tortillas and sprinkle with Jack cheese. Fold burrito-style. Place seam side down in a 13 × 9 baking dish. Pour cream of mushroom soup over top, sprinkle with cheddar cheese, green onions and olives. Cover and bake in a 350° oven for 20 minutes.

Serves 8.

POLLO BURRITOS

3 cups cubed cooked **Chicken**
1 **Onion**, diced
2 cloves **Garlic**, minced
1 can (10.75 oz.) **Cream of Mushroom Soup**
1/2 tsp. **Oregano**
1/4 tsp. **Pepper**
6 large **Flour Tortillas**
1 cup shredded **Monterey Jack Cheese**
1 can (15 oz.) **Enchilada Sauce**
1/2 cup shredded **Cheddar Cheese**
1/2 cup sliced **Green Onions**
Sour Cream

In a large saucepan combine chicken, onion, garlic, soup and seasonings. Cover and simmer over medium heat for 15 minutes. Spoon onto warmed flour tortillas, sprinkle with Jack cheese and fold burrito-style, placing seam side down in a 13 × 9 baking dish. Pour enchilada sauce over the top, sprinkle with cheddar cheese and onions. Bake at 350° for 10 minutes. Serve with sour cream.

Serves 6.

POLLO VERDE BURRITOS

2 tbsp. **Oil**
1 **Onion**, chopped
1 can (7 oz.) diced **Green Chiles**
3 cups cubed cooked **Chicken**
1 can (10.75 oz.) **Cream of Celery Soup**
1 can (4 oz.) sliced **Black Olives**
6 large **Flour Tortillas**
2 cups shredded Cheddar Cheese
1 can (15 oz.) **Green Chile Enchilada Sauce**

In a skillet, heat oil and sauté onion and green chiles until onion is translucent. Add chicken, soup and black olives and heat thoroughly. Spoon onto warmed flour tortillas, sprinkle on cheese, reserving 1/2 cup. Fold burrito style and place seam side down in a baking dish. Pour enchilada sauce over top, sprinkle with remaining cheese and bake at 350° for 20 minutes.

Serves 6.

BAKED TURKEY BURRITOS

3 cups diced cooked Turkey
1 can (10.75 oz.) **Cream of Mushroom Soup**
1 cup **Sour Cream**
1 can (4 oz.) diced **Green Chiles**
1 can (4 oz.) sliced **Black Olives**
8 large **Flour Tortillas**
1 1/2 cups shredded **Monterey Jack Cheese**
1/2 cup shredded **Cheddar Cheese**

In a large bowl, combine turkey, soup, sour cream, green
chiles and black olives. Spoon onto warmed flour tortillas,
sprinkle with Jack cheese; fold burrito-style and place seam
side down in a 13 × 9 baking dish. Sprinkle with cheddar
cheese. Bake at 350° for 45 minutes.

Serves 8.

TURKEY AND CORN BURRITOS

1 1/2 lbs. **Ground Turkey**
1 **Onion**, chopped
1 **Green Bell Pepper**, chopped
1 can (15 oz.) **Tomatoes**
1 can (15 oz.) **Corn**, drained
1 can (4 oz.) sliced **Black Olives**
1 tbsp. **Chili Powder**
1 tsp. **Garlic Salt**
1 tsp. **Cumin**
8 large Flour Tortillas
1 1/2 cups shredded **Monterey Jack Cheese**
Salsa

In a skillet, sauté turkey with onion and bell pepper until onion is translucent. Add tomatoes, corn, olives and seasonings. Combine thoroughly; cover and simmer for 10 minutes. Spoon onto warmed flour tortillas, sprinkle in cheese and fold burrito-style. Serve with salsa.

Serves 8.

POLLO ROJO BURRITOS

3 cups diced cooked **Chicken**
1 **Onion**, finely chopped
1 can (4 oz.) diced **Green Chiles**
1 can (8 oz.) **Tomato Sauce**
1 can (15 oz.) **Tomatoes**, chopped
8 large **Flour Tortillas**
2 cups shredded **Monterey Jack Cheese**
Sour Cream
Salsa

In a medium saucepan, combine chicken, onion, green chiles, tomato sauce and tomatoes and heat thoroughly. Spoon onto warmed flour tortillas, sprinkle with Jack cheese and fold burrito-style. Serve with sour cream and salsa.

Serves 8.

CHICKEN SALAD BURRITOS

2 cups cubed cooked **Chicken**
2 stalks **Celery**, diced
3 **Green Onions**, chopped
2 tbsp. **Lemon Juice**
1 cup shredded **Monterey Jack Cheese**
3/4 cup **Miracle Whip**®
6 large **Flour Tortillas**
Shredded **Lettuce**
Chopped **Tomatoes**

In a medium bowl, combine chicken, celery, green onions, lemon juice, cheese and Miracle Whip. Spoon onto warmed flour tortillas and fold burrito-style. Serve with shredded lettuce and chopped tomatoes.

Serves 6.

THANKSGIVING BURRITOS

2 tbsp. **Oil**
1 Onion, **diced**
2 cups diced cooked **Turkey**
2 cups **Leftover Stuffing**
2 cups **Mashed Potatoes**
2 cups **Gravy**
1 can (4 oz.) diced **Green Chiles**
8 large **Flour Tortillas**
2 cups shredded **Cheddar Cheese**

In a skillet, heat oil and sauté onion until translucent. Add turkey, stuffing, mashed potatoes, gravy and green chiles; heat thoroughly, stirring occasionally. Spoon onto warmed flour tortillas, sprinkle with cheddar cheese and fold burrito-style.

Serves 8.

SEAFOOD BURRITOS

SNAPPER BURRITOS

1/4 cup **Oil**
1 **Onion**, chopped
1 lb. **Red Snapper**, cut into 1-inch cubes
1 **Zucchini**, shredded
1 **Carrot**, shredded
6 large **Flour Tortillas**
1 cup shredded **Monterey Jack Cheese**
Shredded **Lettuce**
Salsa

In a skillet, heat oil and sauté onion until translucent. Stir in red snapper, zucchini and carrot. Continue cooking until snapper flakes with a fork. Spoon onto warmed flour tortillas, sprinkle with cheese, lettuce and salsa and fold burrito-style.

Serves 6.

MAZATLAN BURRITOS

1 lb. **Fish Fillets**, cut into 1-inch cubes
2 tbsp. **Lime Juice**
2 tbsp. **Oil**
1 **Onion**, chopped
1 **Green Bell Pepper**, chopped
1 clove **Garlic**, minced
1 **Tomato**, chopped
1/2 cup **Chili Sauce**
6 large **Flour Tortillas**

Drizzle lime juice over fillets and set aside. In a skillet, heat oil and sauté onion, bell pepper and garlic until onion is translucent. Add fish, tomatoes and chili sauce; simmer, uncovered, for 10 minutes or until fish flakes with a fork. Spoon onto warmed burritos and fold burrito-style.

Serves 6.

WHAT ARE YOU FISHING FOR?
BURRITOS

1 lb. **Halibut,** cut into 1-inch cubes
1 tbsp. **Lemon Juice**
1 tbsp. **Lime Juice**
1 tbsp. **Oil**
1/2 tsp. **Garlic Salt**
1/4 tsp. **Cumin**
1/4 tsp. **Pepper**
1/4 tsp. **Cayenne**
6 large **Flour Tortillas**
1 cup shredded **Monterey Jack Cheese**
Shredded **Lettuce**
Chopped **Tomatoes**
Sour Cream
Salsa

Place halibut in a shallow baking dish; sprinkle with lemon juice, lime juice, oil and seasonings. Cover and refrigerate for 1-2 hours. Uncover and bake at 425° for 15 minutes. Spoon onto warmed flour tortillas. Sprinkle with cheese, lettuce and tomatoes; fold burrito-style. Serve with sour cream and salsa.

Serves 6.

SALMON AND BLACK BEAN BURRITOS

1/4 cup **Olive Oil**
2 tbsp. **Lemon Juice**
2 cloves **Garlic**, minced
4 tbsp. chopped fresh **Cilantro**
1/2 tsp. **Salt**
1 can (20 oz.) **Crushed Pineapple**
1 **Red Bell Pepper**, diced
1 **Jalapeño**, minced
2 **Green Onions**, chopped
1 1/2 lbs. **Salmon**, cooked and flaked
1 can (15 oz.) **Black Beans**, rinsed
8 large **Flour Tortillas**

In a medium bowl, whisk together olive oil, lemon juice, garlic, cilantro and salt. Add pineapple, red bell pepper, jalapeño and green onions. In a separate bowl, mix salmon and black beans; spoon onto warmed flour tortillas. Top with prepared pineapple salsa and fold tortillas burrito-style.

Serves 8.

BATTER-FRIED SHARK BURRITOS

1 cup **Flour**
1 tbsp. **Garlic Salt**
1 tsp. **Baking Powder**
1 cup **Water**
1 tbsp. **Vinegar**
2 lbs. **Shark Fillets,** cut into 1-inch cubes
Oil
8 large **Flour Tortillas**
Shredded **Lettuce**
Chopped **Tomatoes**
Thousand Island Dressing

In a mixing bowl, combine flour, garlic salt and baking powder. Slowly add water and vinegar and mix well. In a skillet, heat oil. Dip shark cubes into batter and drop carefully into hot oil. Cook for 2-3 minutes or until golden brown. Drain on paper towels. Place fried shark cubes onto warmed flour tortillas, sprinkle with lettuce and tomatoes. Drizzle with dressing. Fold burrito-style.

Serves 8.

SWORDFISH BURRITOS

1/4 cup **Oil**
1/4 cup **Lime Juice**
1 tsp. **Garlic Salt**
1/4 tsp. **Chili Powder**
1/8 tsp. **Cayenne**
2 lbs. **Swordfish Steaks** (1-inch cubes)
8 large **Flour Tortillas**
Shredded **Monterey Jack Cheese**
Shredded **Lettuce**
Chopped **Tomatoes**

In a medium bowl, combine oil, lime juice, garlic salt, chili powder and cayenne. Add cubed swordfish and toss well. Cover and refrigerate for at least 2 hours, stirring several times. Place swordfish cubes on lightly oiled broiler pan and broil for about 3 minutes. Place broiled cubes on warmed flour tortillas. Top with cheese, lettuce and tomatoes. Fold burrito-style.

Serves 8.

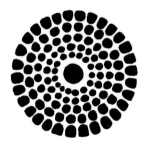

SCALLOPED BURRITOS

1 1/2 lbs. **Scallops**
1/4 cup **Butter**, melted
3 tbsp. **Lemon Juice**
1 tsp. **Garlic Salt**
1/4 tsp. **Pepper**
1/4 tsp. **Cayenne**
3 tbsp. chopped fresh **Cilantro**
8 large **Flour Tortillas**
Shredded **Monterey Jack Cheese**
Shredded **Lettuce**
Sliced **Black Olives**

Rinse scallops under cold running water. Pat dry with paper towels. Arrange scallops on lightly oiled broiler pan. In a small bowl, combine butter, lemon juice, garlic salt, pepper, cayenne and cilantro. Brush scallops with seasoned butter. Broil for 3 minutes; turn scallops, brush with seasoned butter and broil for an additional 3 minutes. Spoon scallops onto warmed flour tortillas; sprinkle with cheese, lettuce and olives. Fold tortillas burrito-style.

Serves 8.

SHRIMP AND FETA BURRITOS

1 lb. cooked **Shrimp**, peeled and deveined
6 lg. flour **Tortillas**
1 cup crumbled **Feta Cheese**
1 lg. **Cucumber,** thinly sliced
2 **Tomatoes,** sliced

Vinaigrette:

4 tsp. **Olive Oil**
3 tbsp. **Lemon Juice**
2 tsp. minced **Garlic**
1/4 tsp. dried **Oregano**
1/2 tsp. dried **Basil**

In a small bowl, combine all vinaigrette ingredients, stir and set aside. Rinse shrimp with cold water; pat dry lightly with paper towels. Brush tortillas with 2 teaspoons of vinaigrette. Sprinkle 2/3 cup feta cheese equally on top of tortillas, hold remaining cheese. Broil just until cheese melts. Arrange cucumber and tomato slices on tortillas. Divide shrimp equally among tortillas and drizzle with remaining vinaigrette. Top with 1/3 cup of remaining feta cheese. Fold burrito-style.

Serves 6.

VEGETARIAN BURRITOS

CARLSBAD BURRITOS

2 tbsp. **Oil**
1 cup sliced **Red Onion**
2 cups **Broccoli Florets**
1 cup sliced **Carrots**
1 cup sliced **Red Bell Pepper**
1 cup sliced fresh **Mushrooms**
1/2 tsp. **Garlic Salt**
1/2 tsp. **Oregano**
1/4 tsp. **Chili Powder**
6 large **Flour Tortillas**
2 cups shredded **Longhorn Cheese**

Heat oil in a large skillet, add onions, broccoli, carrots, red bell pepper and mushrooms and sauté for 2-3 minutes. Add seasonings and sauté an additional 2-3 minutes. Spoon onto warmed flour tortillas, sprinkle with cheese and fold burrito-style. Place burritos seam side down on ungreased cookie sheet; bake at 350° for 5 minutes.

Serves 6.

SPINACH BROCCOLI BURRITOS

1-2 tbsp. **Oil**
1 **Onion**, chopped
1 **Jalapeño**, minced (optional)
1 pkg. (10 oz.) frozen chopped **Spinach**, thawed and
    drained
1 1/2 cups **Broccoli Florets**
1 cup shredded **Longhorn Cheese**
8 oz. **Ricotta Cheese**
1 cup **Salsa**
1/2 tsp. **Garlic Salt**
1/2 tsp. **Oregano**
8 large **Flour Tortillas**

Heat oil in a large skillet, add onion and jalapeño and sauté
until onion is translucent. Add spinach and broccoli;
continue cooking for 5 minutes. Remove from heat and add
1/2 cup shredded cheese, ricotta cheese, 1/2 cup salsa, garlic
salt and oregano; combine thoroughly. Spoon onto warmed
flour tortillas and fold burrito-style. Place burritos seam side
down in a baking dish. Pour remaining salsa over burritos and
sprinkle with remaining cheese. Bake at 325° for 10 minutes.

Serves 8.

SPINACH BURRITOS

1 pkg. (10 oz.) frozen chopped **Spinach**, thawed and
drained
1 can (10.75 oz.) **Cream of Mushroom Soup**
1 ctn. (16 oz.) **Dry Curd Cottage Cheese**
1 can (4 oz.) diced **Green Chiles**
1 cup minced **Onion**
8 large **Flour Tortillas**
3 cups shredded **Cheddar Cheese**

In a large mixing bowl, combine spinach, soup, cottage
cheese, green chiles and onion. Spoon onto warmed flour
tortillas, sprinkle with cheddar cheese, reserving 1 cup. Fold
tortillas burrito-style and place seam side down in a 13 × 9
baking dish. Sprinkle remaining cheese over top. Bake at 325°
for 30 minutes.

Serves 8.

Wrap It Up!

*Wraps, which have recently gained in popularity, are
really nothing more than modern burritos. Today's
wrap cafes and restaurants serve a variety of fillings in
tortillas, pita breads or other edible wrappers. With the
fantastic variety of tortillas now available in stores, feel
free to experiment with the different fillings in this
book to find your favorite flavor combinations!*

BURRITOS OLÉ!

2 tbsp. **Oil**
1 **Onion**, chopped
1 clove **Garlic**, minced
2 **Carrots**, thinly sliced
2 stalks **Celery**, thinly sliced
3 **Zucchini**, thinly sliced
1 **Red Bell Pepper**, chopped
1/2 tsp. **Cumin**
1/2 tsp. **Oregano**
1/2 tsp. **Salt**
1 can (15 oz.) **Kidney Beans**, drained
1 can (15 oz.) **Corn**, drained
8 large **Flour Tortillas**
2 cups shredded **Monterey Jack Cheese**

Heat oil in a large skillet, add onion, garlic, carrots, celery, zucchini and red bell pepper. Cook for 5 minutes, add seasonings and cook an additional 5 minutes. Add kidney beans and corn; cover and simmer for 5 minutes. Spoon onto warmed flour tortillas, sprinkle with cheese and fold burrito-style. If desired, serve with salsa and sour cream.

Serves 8.

POTATO CHILE BURRITOS

2 tbsp. **Oil**
2 cups cubed **Potatoes**
1 can (4 oz.) diced **Green Chiles**
1 can (10.75 oz.) **Cream of Mushroom Soup**
1/2 cup **Water**
3 **Green Onions**, sliced
1/2 tsp. **Chili Powder**
4 large **Flour Tortillas**
1 cup shredded **Cheddar Cheese**
Shredded **Lettuce**
Chopped **Tomatoes**

Heat oil in a large skillet; add potatoes and fry until brown. Add green chiles, soup, water, green onions and chili powder. Heat thoroughly, stirring occasionally. Spoon onto warmed flour tortillas, sprinkle with cheese, lettuce and tomatoes. Fold burrito-style.

Serves 4.

HOMINY BURRITOS

2 tbsp. **Flour**
2 tbsp. **Oil**
1 **Onion**, chopped
1 **Green Bell Pepper**, chopped
1 can (4 oz.) diced **Green Chiles**
1 **Tomato**, chopped
1 can (29 oz.) **Hominy**, drained
1 cup **Water**
1/2 tsp. **Garlic Salt**
1/2 tsp. **Oregano**
1/4 tsp. **Pepper**
8 large **Flour Tortillas**
2 cups shredded **Cheddar Cheese**

In a large skillet, brown flour in oil; add onion and sauté. Add bell pepper, chiles and tomato and continue cooking over medium heat. Stir in hominy, water and seasonings. Cover and simmer for 15 minutes over medium heat, stirring occasionally. Spoon onto warmed flour tortillas, sprinkle with cheese and fold burrito-style.

Serves 8.

HOMINY BEAN BURRITOS

1 can (15 oz.) **Hominy**, drained
1 **Tomato**, chopped
1 can (4 oz.) diced **Green Chiles**
1/2 tsp. **Garlic Salt**
1/2 tsp. **Cumin**
1/2 tsp. **Oregano**
1 can (15 oz.) **Black Beans**, rinsed
6 large **Whole-Wheat Tortillas**

In a saucepan, combine hominy, tomato, chiles and seasonings. Simmer for 10 minutes to allow hominy to absorb flavors. Add black beans and heat thoroughly. Spoon onto warmed flour tortillas and fold burrito-style.

Serves 6.

Hominy Facts

Hominy is corn kernels that have been dried, soaked in a solution of lye and water (changed out several times), and the hard outer shell has been sloughed off. After thorough and repeated washing the hominy is then ready to can or dry.

Bean and Tofu Burritos

10 oz. **Firm Tofu**, cubed
Soy Sauce
1 **Onion**, chopped
2 cloves **Garlic**, minced
2 tbsp. **Oil**
2 cups cooked cubed **Potatoes**
1 can (15 oz.) **Black Beans**, rinsed
1 can (4 oz.) diced **Green Chiles**
1/2 tsp. **Oregano**
1/2 tsp. **Chili Powder**
Salt and **Pepper**
8 large **Flour Tortillas**

Place tofu in a shallow bowl and drizzle soy sauce over top; set aside. In a heated skillet, sauté onion and garlic in oil, until onion is translucent. Add tofu; stir-fry until tofu has developed a lightly browned outer shell. Add potatoes, beans, chiles and seasonings. Continue cooking for 10 minutes, stirring occasionally. Spoon onto warmed flour tortillas and fold burrito-style.

Serves 8.

TOFU AND RICE BURRITOS

2 tbsp. **Oil**
1 **Onion**, chopped
1 **Green Bell Pepper**, chopped
10 oz. **Firm Tofu**, cubed
1/2 tsp. **Garlic Salt**
1 cup **Salsa**
6 large **Whole-Wheat Tortillas**
2 cups cooked **Rice**
1 **Tomato**, chopped
1 **Avocado**, sliced

Heat oil in a skillet and sauté onion and green bell pepper. Add tofu and garlic salt and continue to sauté until tofu is browned. Stir in salsa and heat thoroughly. Spoon onto warmed tortillas. Top each with rice, tomato and avocado. Fold burrito-style. If desired, serve with shredded lettuce and additional salsa.

Serves 6.

Avocados in the United States

While the avocado originated in Central America, commercial cultivation of avocados in the U.S. began in California and Florida in the late 1800's.

SPICY GARDEN BURRITOS

2 tbsp. **Oil**
1 **Red Onion**, chopped
1 **Green Bell Pepper**, chopped
2 cloves **Garlic**, minced
1 can (15 oz.) **Corn**, drained
1 can (15 oz.) **Pinto Beans**, drained
1 cup **Peas**
1/4 cup chopped fresh **Cilantro**
1 tsp. **Hot Sauce**
1/2 tsp. **Chili Powder**
Salt and **Pepper**
6 large **Whole-Wheat Tortillas**

Heat oil in a skillet and sauté onion, green bell pepper and garlic. Stir in corn, beans, peas, cilantro, hot sauce, chili powder, salt and pepper. Heat thoroughly, allowing flavors to blend. Spoon onto warmed flour tortillas and fold burrito-style.

Serves 6.

Cilantro-Love it or Hate it?

Cilantro is a spicy herb that is actually the leaves of the coriander plant. While some people swear by its strong flavor, others swear at it. If you haven't cooked with cilantro before, we suggest that you use small amounts until you determine what your own tastebuds can handle!

CORNY BURRITOS

1 tbsp. **Oil**
1 **Onion**, chopped
1 can (15 oz.) **Corn**, drained
1 can (15 oz.) **Black Beans**, rinsed
1 **Jalapeño**, finely minced
1 tsp. **Oregano**
1/2 tsp. **Garlic Salt**
1/2 tsp. **Pepper**
1 **Avocado**
2 tsp. **Lemon Juice**
2 tbsp. **Salsa**
6 large **Whole-Wheat Tortillas**

In a skillet, heat oil and sauté onion until translucent. Add corn, black beans, jalapeño, oregano, garlic salt and pepper. Heat thoroughly. In a small bowl, mash avocado with lemon juice and stir in salsa. Spread avocado onto warmed tortillas, followed by corn/bean mixture, and fold burrito-style.

Serves 6.

CARROT AND NAVY BEAN BURRITOS

1 tbsp. **Oil**
3 **Carrots**, sliced
1 clove **Garlic**, minced
1 can (15 oz.) **Navy Beans**, drained
1 can (15 oz.) **Mexican Stewed Tomatoes**
1 tsp. **Cumin**
4 large **Flour Tortillas**

In a skillet, heat oil and sauté carrots and garlic until carrots are tender. Add beans, tomatoes and cumin. Simmer for 10 minutes to allow flavors to blend and mixture to thicken. Spoon onto warmed tortillas and fold burrito-style.

Serves 4.

HEART SMART BURRITOS

2 cups **Corn**
1 cup **Peas**
10 Oz. **Firm Tofu**, crumbled
1 can (15 oz.) **Black Beans**, rinsed
1 can (4 oz.) diced **Green Chiles**
1 1/2 cups **Salsa**
6 large **Flour Tortillas**
Shredded **Lettuce**
Chopped **Tomatoes**

Combine first six ingredients in a saucepan and simmer for 15 minutes, stirring occasionally. Spoon onto warmed tortillas; top with lettuce and tomatoes. Fold burrito-style.

Serves 6.

Flat Bread Around the World

There are more than 60 types of flat bread made around the world. They fall into two categories, leavened and unleavened. Tortillas, made from corn or wheat flour, are considered to be round, unleavened bread.

BLACK BEANS AND BROWN RICE BURRITOS

1 can (15 oz.) **Black Beans**, rinsed
1 **Onion**, finely grated
1 can (4 oz.) diced **Green Chiles**
1 can (4 oz.) sliced **Black Olives**
2 tbsp. chopped fresh **Cilantro**
1 tsp. **Chili Powder**
Salt and **Pepper**
8 large **Whole-Wheat Tortillas**
2 cups cooked **Brown Rice**
1 cup **Salsa**

In a large mixing bowl, mash beans with onion; stir in chiles, olives, cilantro, chili powder, salt and pepper. Spoon bean mixture onto warmed tortillas, top with brown rice and fold burrito-style. Place burritos seam side down in a baking dish, pour salsa evenly over top and bake at 350° for 20 minutes.

Serves 8.

SWEET POTATO AND GARBANZO BEAN BURRITOS

2 tbsp. **Oil**
1 **Onion**, chopped
2 cloves **Garlic**, minced
2 cans (15 oz. ea.) **Garbanzo Beans**, drained
1 cup **Salsa**
4 cups mashed cooked **Sweet Potatoes**
2 tbsp. **Butter**
1 tbsp. **Brown Sugar**
1/4 tsp. **Cinnamon**
8 large **Whole-Wheat Tortillas**

In a skillet, heat oil and sauté onion and garlic until onion is translucent. Add garbanzo beans and salsa; reduce heat to low, cover and simmer for 15 minutes. While beans are cooking, place sweet potatoes in saucepan and over low heat combine with butter, brown sugar and cinnamon. When beans are tender, mash with potato masher to desired consistency. Spoon a scoop of beans, followed by a scoop of sweet potatoes onto each warmed flour tortilla. Fold tortillas burrito-style.

Serves 8.

TVP BURRITOS

2 tbsp. **Oil**
1 **Onion**, chopped
1 **Green Bell Pepper**, chopped
1 can (4 oz.) diced **Green Chiles**
1 can (15 oz.) **Kidney Beans**
1 pkg. (1.25 oz.) **Taco Seasoning Mix**
1 1/2 cups **Water**
2 cups **TVP** (**Texturized Vegetable Protein**)
6 large **Flour Tortillas**

In a skillet, heat oil and sauté onion and green bell pepper until onion is translucent. Add green chiles and kidney beans. Stir in taco seasoning mix, water and TVP. Cover and simmer for 15 minutes. Stir occasionally, adding more water if necessary. Spoon onto warmed tortillas and fold burrito-style.

Serves 6.

TVP

Texturized Vegetable Protein (TVP) is made from soy products containing protein. Textured soy will maintain its meaty texture after it has been soaked in water and cooked. As a meat substitute, the most common form or size is as a dry granule, which is rehydrated prior to use. It has a protein content similar to many meats. It also is easy to cook with as it is very bland and adopts the flavors of whatever you are seasoning it with.

Five Pepper Burritos

2 tbsp. **Oil**
1 **Onion**, chopped
1 **Green Bell Pepper**, chopped
1 **Red Bell Pepper**, chopped
1 **Yellow Bell Pepper**, chopped
1 **Jalapeño**, sliced
1/2 tsp. **Garlic Salt**
1/2 tsp. **Chili Powder**
1 can (15 oz.) **Vegetarian Refried Beans**
1 can (4 oz.) diced **Green Chiles**
1 cup **Salsa**
6 large **Flour Tortillas**

In a skillet, heat oil and sauté onion, bell peppers, jalapeño and seasonings; cook until vegetables are tender. In a separate saucepan, combine beans, green chiles and salsa; simmer over low heat. Spread beans onto warmed tortillas; scoop pepper mixture on top of beans. Fold tortillas burrito-style.

Serves 6.

ZESTY ZUCCHINI BURRITOS

2 tbsp. **Oil**
1 **Onion**, chopped
3 **Zucchini**, sliced
1 tsp. **Chili Powder**
1/2 tsp. **Garlic Salt**
1/2 tsp. **Oregano**
1/2 tsp. **Cumin**
2 **Tomatoes**, chopped
6 large **Flour Tortillas**
1 cup **Salsa**

In a skillet, heat oil and sauté onion until translucent. Add zucchini and seasonings and continue to sauté until zucchini is crisp-tender. Remove from heat and stir in tomatoes. Spoon onion mixture onto warmed tortillas and fold burrito-style. Place burritos seam side down in a 13 × 9 baking dish. Pour salsa over burritos and bake at 325° for 10 minutes.

Serves 6.

Zucchini

Zucchini has been popular in Central and South America for several thousand years; the zucchini we enjoy today is a variety of summer squash developed in Italy.

DESSERT BURRITOS

CHERRY BURRITOS

2 cans (16 oz. ea.) **Cherry Pie Filling**
12 small **Flour Tortillas**
2 cups **Sugar**
1/2 cup **Butter**
1 cup **Water**
1 tsp. **Cinnamon**
Vanilla Ice Cream

Spoon pie filling onto tortillas, roll and place seam side down in a large casserole dish. In a saucepan, combine 1 1/2 cups sugar, butter and water; bring to a rolling boil. Pour mixture over burritos and let stand for 20 minutes. Combine remaining 1/2 cup sugar with cinnamon and sprinkle over burritos. Bake for 30 minutes at 350°. Serve warm with vanilla ice cream.

Serves 6.

BANANAS FOSTER BURRITOS

1/2 cup **Dark Rum**
1/4 cup **Butter**
1 cup packed **Brown Sugar**
1/2 tsp. **Cinnamon**
4 **Bananas**
8 medium **Flour Tortillas**
Vanilla Ice Cream

In a skillet, over low heat, combine rum, butter, brown sugar and cinnamon, stirring until sugar dissolves. Peel and split bananas lengthwise and then cut in half. Place bananas in butter rum sauce and continue to cook until bananas begin to brown. Lift bananas out of pan, place two pieces on each tortilla. Top with a scoop of vanilla ice cream and roll tortilla, placing seam side down on serving dish. Spoon warm sauce over the top and serve immediately.

Serves 8.

PINEAPPLE PEACH BURRITOS

1 can (15 oz.) **Pineapple Chunks,** drained
1 can (16 oz.) **Peach Pie Filling**
1/3 cup **Brown Sugar**
1/4 cup **Butter**
1/2 tsp. **Cinnamon**
8 medium **Flour Tortillas**
Whipped Cream

In a saucepan, combine pineapple, peach pie filling, brown sugar, butter and cinnamon. Heat thoroughly, stirring occasionally. Spoon onto warmed flour tortillas and roll, placing seam side down on serving dish. Serve with a dollop of whipped cream.

Serves 8.

FRIED FRUIT BURRITOS

1 pkg. (16 oz.) **Dried Fruit Bits**
1/2 cup **Apple Juice**
1/2 tsp. **Cinnamon**
1 tbsp. **Cornstarch**
8 medium **Flour Tortillas**
Oil
Powdered Sugar

In a saucepan, combine fruit, apple juice, cinnamon and cornstarch. Cook on medium heat, stirring until thickened. While heating oil in a frying pan, spoon 1 heaping tablespoon of fruit filling in center of each tortilla; roll tightly. Place rolled burritos in hot oil and fry until brown, turning once. Drain on paper towels. Sprinkle with powdered sugar.

Serves 8.

Apple Raisin Burritos

1/2 cup **Butter**
4 **Apples**, peeled, cored and sliced
1/2 cup **Raisins**
1/3 cup **Sugar**
1 tsp. **Cinnamon**
8 medium **Flour Tortillas**
Whipped Cream

In a skillet, melt butter; add apple slices, raisins, sugar and cinnamon. Cook over medium heat until apples begin to soften. Spoon onto flour tortillas and roll; place seam side down on serving plate. Top with a dollop of whipped cream.

Serves 8.

EASY APPLE BURRITOS

3 **Apples**, cored and sliced
1/2 cup **Sugar**
1/2 tsp. **Cinnamon**
1/2 tsp. **Nutmeg**
6 medium **Flour Tortillas**

In a mixing bowl, mix apple slices with sugar, cinnamon and nutmeg. Spread apples on tortillas, fold burrito style and heat in microwave oven on High for 1 minute. Place on serving dish and serve with ice cream, whipped cream or powdered sugar.

Serves 6.

INDEX

Recipe:_____

From:_____

Ingredients:

_____   _____

_____   _____

_____   _____

_____   _____

_____   _____

Directions:_____

_____

_____

_____

_____

Recipe:_____

From:_____

Ingredients:

_____   _____

_____   _____

_____   _____

_____   _____

_____   _____

Directions:_____

_____

_____

_____

_____

Recipe:_____

From:_____

Ingredients:

_____   _____

_____   _____

_____   _____

_____   _____

_____   _____

Directions:_____

_____

_____

_____

_____

Recipe:_____

From:_____

Ingredients:

_____   _____

_____   _____

_____   _____

_____   _____

_____   _____

Directions:_____

_____

_____

_____

_____

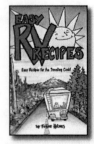

QTY	TITLE	PRICE	TOTAL
	Burrito Lovers' Cook Book	9.95	
	Chili Lovers' Cook Book	9.95	
	Chip & Dip Lovers' Cook Book	9.95	
	Citrus Lovers' Cook Book	9.95	
	Easy BBQ Recipes	9.95	
	Easy BBQ Sauces	9.95	
	Grand Canyon Cook Book	9.95	
	Low Fat Mexican Recipes	9.95	
	New Mexico Cook Book	9.95	
	Mexican Family Favorites Cook Book	9.95	
	Quick-n-Easy Mexican Recipes	9.95	
	Salsa Lovers' Cook Book	9.95	
	Sedona Cook Book	9.95	
	Tequila Cook Book	9.95	
	Texas Cook Book	9.95	
	Tortilla Lovers' Cook Book	9.95	
	Veggie Lovers' Cook Book	9.95	
	Western Breakfast	9.95	

US Shipping & Handling Add — 1-3 Books: 5.00
[for non-domestic ship rates, please call] — 4-9 Books: 7.00
9+ Books: 7.00 + 0.25 per book
AZ residents add 8.3% sales tax

(US funds only) Total:

Please make checks payable to:
Golden West Publishers
4113 N. Longview,
Phoenix, AZ 85014

☐ Check or money order enclosed
☐ MC ☐ VISA ☐ Discover ☐ American Express Verification Code:_____

Card Number:_____ Exp._____
Signature: _____
Name_____Phone:_____
Address _____
City_____State_____ZIP _____
Email _____

Prices are subject to change.

Visit our website or call us toll free for a free catalog of all our titles!